12 Mini French Plays

Use Drama to Develop Pupils' Confidence in Speaking, Listening, Reading and Writing French

2nd edition

Danièle Bourdais and Sue Finnie

> **For instructions on how to download your free audio files and printable resources for the plays, please see page 49.**

We hope you and your pupils enjoy performing the mini-plays in this book.

Brilliant Publications publishes many other books for teaching modern foreign languages.

To find out more details on any of our titles, please go to our website: www.brilliantpublications.co.uk.

Written by Danièle Bourdais and Sue Finnie
Illustrated by Chris McLeod
Editorial, design and production by Hart McLeod Ltd.
Front cover designed by Brilliant Publications Limited
Audio recorded by Hart McLeod Ltd at Goldman Associates Audioworks, Cambridge
Voiced by Fernando Tiberini, Liz Dall'Aglio, Sophia Dall'Aglio and Samy Hamdane
Additional music provided by Stuart Finnie, Duncan Menzies and Gordozo Murch

© Text Danièle Bourdais and Sue Finnie 2010
© Design Brilliant Publications Limited 2010

Print: ISBN 978-1-78317-360-0
pdf: ISBN 978-1-78317-361-7

First printed and published in the UK in 2010, 2nd edition 2024
First edition title: 12 Petites Pièces à Jouer

The right of Danièle Bourdais and Sue Finnie to be identified as the authors of this work has been asserted by themselves in accordance with the Copyright, Designs and Patents Act 1988.

All rights reserved. Apart from any use permitted under UK copyright law, no part of this publication may be reproduced or transmitted in any form or by any means, electronic or mechanical, including photocopying and recording, or held within any information storage and retrieval system, without permission in writing from the publishers or under licence from the Copyright Licensing Agency Limited. Further details of such licenses (for reprographic reproduction) may be obtained from the Copyright Licensing Agency Limited, 5th Floor, Shackleton House, 4 Battle Bridge Lane, London SE1 2HX (https://cla.co.uk)

Published by Brilliant Publications Limited
Unit 10
Sparrow Hall Farm
Edlesborough
Dunstable
Bedfordshire
LU6 2ES, UK

Email: info@brilliantpublications.co.uk
Website: www.brilliantpublications.co.uk

Brilliant Publications is a registered trademark.

Contents

Introduction:
- Why use drama? ... 4
- What is **12 Mini French Plays**? ... 5
- Who are the plays for? ... 5
- Suggestions for use ... 6

1. Au café ... 8
   A difficult customer does nothing but complain

2. Bobo le robot ... 11
   Which inventor has created the best robot?

3. Je veux un bonbon ! ... 13
   Learn to be polite and get your way!

4. Un kilomètre à pied ... 15
   A class-trip to visit a castle proves a long trek

5. Vive le temps d'hiver ! ... 17
   Santa checks the weather in France daily until conditions are right for a visit

6. Qui aime les fantômes ? ... 19
   Having a friendly ghost around the house can be useful

7. J'ai du talent ! ... 22
   Contestants battle it out in a musical talent show

8. Le lièvre et la tortue ... 25
   A French version of the fable The Hare and the Tortoise

9. Le cheval du désert ... 27
   A traditional North African animal tale

10. La ronde des mois ... 29
    A whistle-stop tour of the French year and French celebrations

11. Jacques et le haricot magique ... 31
    The traditional tale of Jack and the Beanstalk revisited in French

12. Vive la Révolution ! ... 34
    The French Revolution – blow by blow!

Activity sheets ... 37
Instructions for downloading digital files ... 49

Introduction

Why use drama?

Dear teacher

Acting is a fun way to practise French. And the good news is that you don't need to be a drama teacher to get the most from it.

There are lots of benefits:
- it's motivating – pupils love it
- it adds variety to lessons
- it promotes fluency – pupils understand and retain language easily
- it allows you to explore different cultures, historical periods, etc
- it's multi-sensory and inclusive
- it offers opportunities for cross-curricular work
- it helps embed good language learning practices

Enjoyment

Pupils enjoy themselves as they would in their own language. Performing 'a staged play' helps justify the use of a different language.

Improved confidence

Pupils learn to value their own contribution and understand their role within a group. Shy children often enjoy performing when wearing masks and costumes.

End-product

Performances at assemblies, Christmas shows, etc provide children (and the school) with an opportunity to 'show off' their foreign language skills. Video a performance where possible. Why not also post it on your school website or exchange it with a partner school abroad if you have one?

Linguistic objectives

- Drama allows children to develop a range of skills useful for successful language learning:
  - listening skills
  - reading skills
  - expressive reading/speaking
  - memorizing through listening and repetition, etc.

- Pupils discover and use in another language vocabulary they are already familiar with in their mother tongue (days, months, animals, food items, etc).

- Children practise natural intonation (exclamation, interrogation, etc) and pronunciation (liaisons, etc) without the need for pronunciation drills.

- Playlets can stimulate children's own natural creativity, so that they invent new scenes or write their own very simple playlets closely based on what they have done in class.

MFL and drama have a lot in common – in both, pupils need to be active, expressive and to communicate.

There are obvious links you can make with literacy, but you'll also find opportunities for links with other areas of the curriculum (history, music, habitats, countries, festivals, and so on).

Treat drama in French lessons as an exciting adventure. Your enthusiasm will inspire pupils.

Have fun! Danièle and Sue

What is 12 Mini French Plays?

A pack of 12 short plays for pupils to act out in class, working in groups (or, in some cases, as a whole class).

For instructions on how to download your free printable resources and audio files of the plays acted by native-speaker actors, with sound effects, please see page 49.

For each play, there is a Teacher's page with:

- a vocabulary list
- a list of grammar and functions
- details of useful props/costumes/sets/number of actors
- specific language or culture notes
- an English translation of the play.

There is also a printable Activity sheet to go with each play (see pages 37–48).

Who are the plays for?

The plays are aimed at KS2 pupils (Years 3–6) learning French, but are also suitable for KS3 pupils in Year 7 (in order to ease transition between primary and secondary schools).

The plays in this pack are:

- age-appropriate, written for beginners
- short with simple, repetitive language
- designed to be flexible, involving the whole group, no matter how big or how small. For example, a narrator part may be split among several pupils or read from a script; crowds or groups can be composed of any number of children
- ideal for catering for differentiation: children can do as much/as little as they are able or willing to do, from acting out the text to colouring a prop, for example, according to their abilities and interest
- great for mixed-ability groups, as there are roles for all – even those with non-speaking or minimal speaking parts will benefit from listening to others
- written to reinforce language pupils are learning and which is 'really useful' so it can be transferred to all sorts of 'real-life' situations
- an ideal way to deliver many of the KS2 Programmes of Study for Languages: listen attentively to spoken language and show understanding by joining and responding; develop accurate pronunciation and intonation; read carefully and show understanding of words, phrases and simple writing; and broaden their vocabulary and develop their ability to understand new words that are introduced into familiar written material
- made up of manageable chunks of language – no long speeches!
- full of opportunities for developing gestures, emotion and expression
- written to include a song or possible sound effects to add to the fun.

    There are some indications for staging but we suggest teachers and pupils discuss and make up their own (eg how far do you go with the guillotine scene in the French Revolution play?!).

Suggestions for use

1 Choose a suitable play

Plays are arranged in approximate order of difficulty (see Contents list). The first few are more suitable for beginners, the later ones for pupils with more language under their belts.

Your choice can be based on interest – what will motivate your particular group? – or relevance (working on festivals? Choose *La ronde des mois*; working on the life of a plant? Choose *Jacques et le haricot magique*).

Pupils need to be familiar with most of the language of a play before they act it out.

Use a play to reinforce language already learned in class or to pre-teach key words and expressions.

2 Listen to the audio version (see page 49 for instructions on how to download the free audio files)

Pupils can listen without scripts at first (this provides opportunities for listening comprehension/discussion of what's happening).

Use the audio version too for pupils:

- to read along as they listen (this will help them to make sound-spelling links)
- to close their eyes and visualize the action
- to hear a model of good pronunciation, with actors speaking expressively
- in preparation for using the worksheets.

Ideally, find reasons to listen several times, at various stages in the production of your play.

3 Allocate roles

Children can work in small groups or as a whole class. It is important that each child has a role which matches his/her ability level (ie what they can cope with so that they will be successful in what they do). Playlets let every member of the class become involved but allow for differentiation, so that children can do as much or as little as they are able or willing to do, from playing the lead to saying a few words or joining in a chorus. They may also help by making a prop for example, or directing the action or acting as prompter, according to their abilities and interest.

Remember that where there is a narrator's part, it can be broken down and shared among several children.

Print out scripts and hand out a copy to each child. Each person could highlight their part with a highlighter pen. Where a masculine/feminine choice is given, children should cross out the one that doesn't apply.

4 Prepare

Always allow plenty of preparation/rehearsal time, to avoid pupils feeling stressed.

Start by discussing with the group practical issues and how best to stage the show, eg think about sound effects: will they be recorded, or provided by a 'sound crew' (two or three children making the sounds with their voices)?

Try to abandon reading from the scripts as soon as possible. Focus on movement and gestures.

Stress that to be successful, children need to take part with enthusiasm, respect others and work together/co-operate.

Help with learning lines:

- Pupils can perform with or without their scripts – ideally learning their parts by heart – with one child in the group acting as prompter.
- Use facial expressions and gestures.
- Get pupils to listen and say their part in their head or mime to the audio first.
- Use the Activity sheets to help familiarize pupils with the key language, if appropriate.
- Video a rehearsal and let pupils watch and suggest ways to improve their performance.
- Practise little and often.

Be creative:

- The playlets can stimulate children's own natural creativity: let them invent new scenes or write their own very simple playlets closely based on what they have done in class.
- Have pupils draw up a storyboard or PowerPoint version of the story, with captions, to show where characters stand, their facial expressions, etc.
- Let pupils make posters to advertise their performance, or invitations for parents.

Pupils could research and make props and sound effects. YouTube can be a good source of background music.

5 Perform the play!

It is really important to perform the play to an audience – either to other groups in the class, to another class in your school or to parents, in order for pupils' efforts to be rewarded.

It is a good idea to start the performance with a song or similar warm-up activity, to get pupils used to being on stage.

Video the performance where possible, so pupils can watch it later.

The plays are short and it is quite OK to perform them to non-French speakers (eg as a class assembly or performance to parents) as the gestures and actions will convey the meaning. It can even be turned into a virtue if you ask pupils to bear this in mind and make their performance especially expressive!

To help non-linguists, it is also a good idea to provide a programme with the script and English translation (as provided on the Teacher's page) alongside.

1. Au café

Teacher's page

Vocabulary:	Vous désirez ?; je voudrais une pizza/ une portion de frites/un verre d'eau/ un verre propre/l'addition; voilà; bon appétit !; merci; s'il vous plaît; il y a un problème ?; c'est trop petit/trop salé/sale	**Props:**	Menu; notepad; 2 plates (one with a pizza, one with chips – these could be drawn onto paper plates); 2 glasses of water; five one euro coins; tablecloth and cutlery, if wanted
Functions:	Asking someone what they want; ordering food and drink; attracting attention in a café; asking if there is a problem; explaining a problem; wishing someone a good meal	**Sound effects:**	None
		Costumes:	Apron for waiter/waitress
		Set:	Café setting: table and chairs
		Chorus possible:	No
Grammar	Je voudrais + noun; c'est (trop) + adjective		
Characters	2 (waiter/waitress, customer)		

Notes

- Encourage pupils to extend the playlet by adding in more things for the customer to complain about: cold soup, dry bread, etc.

Translation

At the café

Waiter	Good morning, Sir/Madam. What would you like?
Customer	I'd like a pizza, please.
Waiter	A pizza … very good.
Customer	Thank you.
Waiter	Here's your pizza. Enjoy your meal!
Customer	Thank you.
Customer	Oh blast! Excuse me …
Waiter	Yes, Sir/Madam. Is there a problem?
Customer	Yes, the pizza … It's too small. I'd like a portion of chips too.
Waiter	A portion of chips … very good.
Customer	Thank you.
Waiter	Here's your portion of chips. Enjoy your meal!
Customer	Thank you.
Customer	Oh blast! Excuse me …
Waiter	Yes, Sir/Madam. Is there a problem?
Customer	Yes! The chips are too salty. I'd like a glass of water too.
Waiter	A glass of water … very good.
Customer	Thank you.
Waiter	Here's your glass of water. Enjoy your meal!
Customer	Thank you.
Customer	Oh blast! Excuse me …
Waiter	Yes, Sir/Madam. Is there a problem?
Customer	Yes! The glass is dirty. I'd like a clean glass.
Waiter	A clean glass … very good.
Customer	Thank you.
Waiter	Here's your clean glass. Enjoy your meal!
Customer	Thank you.
Customer	Excuse me …
Waiter	Yes, Sir/Madam. Is there a problem?
Customer	No, no, no! I'd like the bill, please
Waiter	Here's the bill. That will be nine euros.
Customer	One … two … three … four … five … Excuse me …
Waiter	Yes, Sir/Madam. Is there a problem?
Customer	Er, yes … I haven't got nine euros. I've got five euros.
Waiter	Dear, oh dear! Off to the kitchen! You'll have to do the washing-up!

1. Au café

A customer is seated at a café table reading the menu. The waiter/waitress approaches. The customer is rather pompous. The waiter/waitress is polite.

Waiter (to customer) Bonjour, Monsieur (or Madame). Vous désirez ?
Customer Je voudrais une pizza, s'il vous plaît.
Waiter (writing on pad) Une pizza ... très bien.
Customer Merci.

Waiter goes off.

Waiter (returns with pizza on a plate) Une pizza, voilà. Bon appétit !
Customer Merci.

Waiter goes off.

Customer (looks at pizza, disappointed) Ah zut !
(raises hand to call waiter) S'il vous plaît ...
Waiter (goes to customer) Oui, Monsieur (or Madame) ? Il y a un problème ?
Customer (points to pizza) Oui ! La pizza, c'est trop petit. Je voudrais aussi une portion de frites.

Waiter (writing on pad) Une portion de frites ... très bien.
Customer Merci.

Waiter goes off.

Waiter (returns with chips on a plate) Une portion de frites, voilà. Bon appétit !
Customer Merci.

Waiter goes off.

Customer (tastes a chip, looks disappointed) Ah zut !
(raises hand to call waiter) S'il vous plaît ...
Waiter (goes to customer) Oui, Monsieur (or Madame) ? Il y a un problème ?
Customer (points to chips) Oui ! Les frites, c'est trop salé. Je voudrais aussi un verre d'eau.
Waiter (writing on pad) Un verre d'eau ... très bien.
Customer Merci.

Waiter goes off.

Waiter (returns with glass of water) Un verre d'eau, voilà. Bon appétit !
Customer Merci.

Waiter goes off.

Customer *(looks at glass, disappointed)* Ah zut !
(raises hand to call waiter) S'il vous plaît …
Waiter *(goes to customer, starting to get annoyed)* Oui, Monsieur (or Madame) ? Il y a un problème ?
Customer *(points to glass)* Oui ! Le verre, c'est sale. Je voudrais un verre propre.
Waiter *(struggling to be polite)* Un verre propre … très bien.
Customer Merci.

Waiter goes off.

Waiter *(returns with second glass)* Un verre propre … voilà. Bon appétit !
Customer Merci.

Waiter goes off.

Customer *(eats and drinks and finishes meal)*
(raises hand to call waiter) S'il vous plaît …
Waiter *(goes to customer, annoyed)* Oui, Monsieur (or Madame) ? Il y a un problème ?
Customer *(shakes head)* Non, non, non ! Je voudrais l'addition, s'il vous plaît.
Waiter *(goes off and comes back with the bill)* Voilà l'addition. Ça fait neuf euros.

Waiter goes off.

Customer *(searches in wallet)*
(counts out coins one by one) Un … deux … trois … quatre … cinq …
(sheepishly raises hand to call waiter)
S'il vous plaît …
Waiter *(goes to customer, really annoyed)* Oui, Monsieur (or Madame) ?
Il y a un problème ?
Customer Euh, oui … Je n'ai pas neuf euros …
j'ai cinq euros.
Waiter *(holds head in despair, then points to kitchen)*
Oh là là ! À la cuisine ! Vous allez faire la
vaisselle !

Customer slinks off to kitchen, head down in disgrace.

2. Bobo le robot

Teacher's page

Vocabulary:	Verbs of movement; bonjour; au revoir; voici … ; écoute; regarde; s'il vous plaît; ça suffit
Functions:	Giving instructions; saying hello/goodbye; introducing someone/thing
Grammar	Imperatives; regular –er verbs (je form)
Characters	4 (2 inventors and 2 robots)
Props:	None
Sound effects:	Crackles, fizzes and other electronic noises as robots are switched on; bang or explosion at the end
Costumes:	Mask or cardboard box painted silver for robots; white coats for inventors
Set:	Science laboratory
Chorus possible:	No

Notes

- Pupils could record their own sound effects or you could appoint a 'sound crew' (two or three pupils to make the sounds with their voices).
- The instructions the inventors give their robots are also useful classroom commands which you could use regularly with pupils.

Translation

Bobo the robot

Inventor 1	Hello! I am an inventor.
Inventor 2	Hello! I am an inventor too!
Inventor 1	I have invented a robot … Here is my robot!
Inventor 2	I have invented a robot too … Here is my robot!
Inventor 1	I'm switching on my robot.
Robot 1	He—llo! I am a robot. My name is Bobo.
Inventor 2	I'm switching on my robot too.
Robot 2	He—llo! I am a robot. My name is Toto.
Inventor 1	Bobo … listen!
Robot 1	I'm listening!
Inventor 1	Bobo … walk!
Robot 1	I'm walking!
Inventor 1	Bobo … stop!
Robot 1	I'm stopping!
Inventor 1	My robot is great, isn't it?
Inventor 2	Hmmm … Toto … look!
Robot 2	I'm looking!
Inventor 2	Toto … sit down!
Robot 2	I'm sitting down!
Inventor 2	Toto … get up!
Robot 2	I'm getting up!
Inventor 2	And what about my robot? Great, isn't it?
Inventor 1	Hmmm!
Robot 1	Bobo … the robot … great … great …
Robot 2	Toto … the robot … great … great …
Inventor 1	No, no, please, that's enough, robots!
Inventor 2	No, no, please. Toto, Bobo, that's enough!
Inventor 1	Oh dear! Goodbye, Bobo!
Inventor 2	Oh dear! Goodbye, Toto!
Inventors 1 and 2	Robots, huh! Goodbye!

2. Bobo le robot

The two inventors are standing either side of the stage, each with their robot at their side.

Inventor 1 (*steps forward and speaks to audience*) Bonjour ! Moi, je suis inventeur.
Inventor 2 (*does the same*) Bonjour ! Moi aussi, je suis inventeur !
Inventor 1 (*points to his/her Robot*) J'ai inventé un robot … Voici mon robot !
Inventor 2 (*points to his/her Robot*) Moi aussi, j'ai inventé un robot … Voici mon robot !
Inventor 1 (*switches Robot on – electronic noises*) J'allume mon robot.
Robot 1 (*making jerky movements*) Bon – jour ! Je suis un robot. Je m'appelle Bobo.
Inventor 2 (*switches Robot on – electronic noises*) Moi aussi, j'allume mon robot.
Robot 2 (*making jerky movements*) Bon – jour ! Je suis un robot. Je m'appelle Toto.
Inventor 1 (*touches his/her ear and speaks to Robot*) Bobo … écoute !
Robot 1 (*copying gesture*) J'écoute !
Inventor 1 (*to Robot*) Bobo … marche !
Robot 1 (*walks*) Je marche !
Inventor 1 (*holds up hand to stop walking Robot*) Bobo … arrête-toi !
Robot 1 (*stops*) Je m'arrête !
Inventor 1 (*turns to Inventor 2, proudly*) Génial, mon robot, non ?
Inventor 2 (*touches his/her eyes and speaks to Robot*) Hmmm. … Toto … regarde !
Robot 2 (*copying gesture*) Je regarde !
Inventor 2 (*to Robot, hand gesture down*) Toto … assieds-toi !
Robot 2 (*sits down*) Je m'assieds !
Inventor 2 (*to Robot, hand gesture up*) Toto … lève-toi !
Robot 2 (*stands up*) Je me lève !
Inventor 2 (*turns to Inventor 1, proudly*) Et mon robot ? Génial, non ?
Inventor 1 (*rubs chin, looking doubtful*) Hmmm !

The two Robots start to move around jerkily out of control.

Robot 1 (*speech out of control*) Bobo … le robot … génial … génial…
Robot 2 (*speech out of control*) Toto … le robot … génial … génial…

The two inventors try to stop them.

Inventor 1 (*pleading*) Non, non, s'il vous plaît, ça suffit, les robots !
Inventor 2 (*pleading*) Non, non, s'il vous plaît. Toto, Bobo, ça suffit !

The two Robots collide and fall to the ground with a bang.

Inventor 1 (*shaking head sadly*) Oh là là ! Au revoir, Bobo !
Inventor 2 (*shaking head sadly*) Oh là là ! Au revoir, Toto !
Both inventors (*gesturing with arms*) Les robots, pfff !
(*wave to audience and walk off*) Au revoir !

3. Je veux un bonbon !

Teacher's page

Vocabulary:	Food items (*une banane, une pomme, des biscuits, un bonbon*)
Functions:	Polite requests (*je voudrais … s'il te plaît*); thanking (*merci*)
Grammar	Modal verb *vouloir*: *Je veux/je voudrais*
Characters	5 (3 children, 1 mum, 1 dad)
Props:	Fruit bowl; fruit (with apple and banana); plate; biscuits; bag of sweets
Costumes:	eg scarf (mum), cap (dad)
Sound effects:	None
Set:	A kitchen, with table and chairs
Chorus possible:	No

Notes
- Encourage pupils to use polite forms of address with you and with each other when speaking French.
- Remind pupils to use facial expression and body language to reinforce what is being said.

Translation

I want a sweet!

Scene 1
Child 1 Mum, I want a banana!
Mum No! You must say: 'I'd like a banana, please!'
Child 1 I'd like a banana, please.
Mum Here is a banana. You must say: 'Thank you!' Dear, oh dear, children!

Scene 2
Child 2 Dad, I want an apple!
Dad No! You must say: 'I'd like an apple, please!'
Child 2 I'd like an apple, please.
Dad Here is an apple. You must say: 'Thank you.' Dear oh dear, children!

Scene 3
Child 3 Mum, I want some biscuits!
Mum No! You must say: 'I'd like some biscuits, please!'
Child 3 I'd like some biscuits, please.
Dad Here are some biscuits.
Mum + Dad You must say: 'Thank you.' Dear oh dear, children!

Scene 4
Dad Mmmm! I want a sweet!
Mum Mmmm! I want a sweet!
Child 1 No! You must say: 'I'd like a sweet, please!'
Dad I'd like a sweet, please.
Mum I'd like a sweet, please.
Child 2 Here is a sweet.
Child 3 Here is a sweet.
Children You must say: 'Thank you!' Dear, oh dear, parents!

3. Je veux un bonbon !

Scene 1 Mum and Dad are arranging fruit in a bowl. Child 1 enters.

Child 1 (*stomping foot on floor*) Maman, je veux une banane !

Mum (*disapprovingly*) Non ! On dit: « Je voudrais une banane, s'il te plaît. »

Child 1 (*smiling sweetly*) Je voudrais une banane, s'il te plaît !

Mum (*handing banana to Child 1*) Tiens, une banane.
(*Child 1 grabs banana and sits down at the table*)

Mum (*sighing and rolling eyes up*) On dit: « Merci ! » … Oh là là, les enfants !

Scene 2 Mum and Dad are arranging fruit in a bowl, Child 2 enters.

Child 2 Papa, je veux une pomme !

Dad (*disapprovingly*) Non ! On dit: « Je voudrais une pomme, s'il te plaît. »

Child 2 (*smiling sweetly*) Je voudrais une pomme, s'il te plaît !

Dad (*handing apple to Child*) Tiens, une pomme.
(*Child 2 grabs apple and sits down at table*)

Dad (*sighing and rolling eyes up*) On dit: « Merci ! » … Oh là là, les enfants !

Scene 3 Mum and Dad are putting biscuits on a plate. Child 3 enters.

Child 3 Maman, je veux des biscuits !

Mum (*disapprovingly*) Non ! On dit : « Je voudrais des biscuits, s'il te plaît. »

Child 3 (*smiling sweetly*) Je voudrais des biscuits, s'il te plaît.

Dad (*holding out biscuits to Child 3*) Tiens, des biscuits.
(*Child 3 grabs biscuit and sits down at table*)

Mum + Dad (*laughing and rolling eyes up*) On dit : « Merci. » … Oh là là, les enfants !

Scene 4 Children have taken sweets out of their pockets and are sharing them

Dad Miam-miam ! Je veux un bonbon !

Mum Miam-miam ! Je veux un bonbon !

Child 1 (*disapprovingly*) Non ! On dit: « Je voudrais un bonbon, s'il te plaît. »

Dad (*laughs*) Je voudrais un bonbon, s'il te plaît.

Mum (*laughs*) Je voudrais un bonbon, s'il te plaît.

Child 2 (*giving sweet reluctantly to Dad*) Tiens, un bonbon.

Child 3 (*giving sweet reluctantly to Mum*) Tiens, un bonbon.
(*Mum & Dad grab sweet and leave, laughing*)

Children (*all together, rolling eyes up*) On dit: « Merci ! » … Oh là là, les parents !

4. Un kilomètre à pied

Teacher's page

Vocabulary: On fait une excursion; on va au château; Pour aller au château, s'il vous plaît ?; allez à droite/à gauche/tout droit; on est fatigué; fermé

Functions: Asking someone the way; giving directions; saying thank you

Grammar Imperatives (écoutez, allez)

Characters 6+ (teacher, class (2+ pupils), 3 passers-by)

Props: Fermé sign for the castle door

Costumes: None (French school children do not wear school uniform)

Sound effects: None

Set: A classroom; the countryside; door with Fermé sign for final scene

Chorus possible: Yes (the class can consist of any number of pupils)

Notes
- The song Un kilomètre à pied is well-known to French children. It is a traditional marching song. Teach the song first, before starting on the play.
- Pupils need to march round and round while singing and between scenes. Make sure they get gradually slower and more tired to convey the length of their hike.

Translation

One kilometre on foot

Scene 1
Teacher	Listen, children! Today we are going on a trip. We are going to the castle.
Class	A trip! Great!
Teacher	Let's go!
All (sing)	One kilometre on foot It wears out, it wears out One kilometre on foot It wears out your shoes
Teacher	Excuse me, Sir/Madam? Can you tell me the way to the castle, please?
Passer-by 1	The castle? Go right!
Teacher	Thank you, Sir/Madam. Let's go!
Pupils	It's a long way!

Scene 2
All (sing)	Two kilometres on foot It wears out, it wears out Two kilometres on foot It wears out your shoes
Teacher	Excuse me, Sir/Madam? Can you tell me the way to the castle, please?
Passer-by 2	The castle? Go left!
Teacher	Thank you, Sir/Madam. Let's go!
Pupils	It's a long way!

Scene 3
All (sing)	Three kilometres on foot It wears out, it wears out Three kilometres on foot It wears out your shoes
Teacher	Excuse me, Sir/Madam? Can you tell me the way to the castle, please?
Passer-by 3	The castle? Go straight on!
Teacher	Thank you, Sir/Madam. Let's go!
Pupils	It's a long way!

Scene 4
Class	Where is the castle?
Pupil 1	We're tired!
Pupil 2	It's a long way.
Teacher	Be quiet, children! There's the castle …
Class	It's the castle! Great!
Teacher	Oh no! The castle is shut!

4. Un kilomètre à pied

Scene 1

Teacher	*(to class)*	Écoutez, les enfants ! Aujourd'hui, on fait une excursion. On va au château.
Class	*(excited)*	Une excursion ! Super !
Teacher	On y va !	
All	*(sing as they march round in single file or pairs)*	

Un kilomètre à pied, Ça use, ça use
Un kilomètre à pied, Ça use les souliers.

Teacher Excusez-moi, Monsieur (or Madame). Pour aller au château, s'il vous plaît ?
Passer-by 1 *(points right)* Le château ? Allez à droite.
Teacher Merci, Monsieur (or Madame). *(Says again to pupils)* On y va !
Pupils C'est loin !

Scene 2

All *(sing as they march round)*

Deux kilomètres à pied, Ça use, ça use
Deux kilomètres à pied, Ça use les souliers.

Teacher Excusez-moi, Monsieur (or Madame). Pour aller au château, s'il vous plaît ?
Passer-by 2 *(points left)* Le château ? Allez à gauche.
Teacher Merci, Monsieur (or Madame). *(Says again to pupils)* On y va !
Pupils C'est loin !

Scene 3

All *(sing as they march round, becoming slower and more tired)*

Trois kilomètres à pied, Ça use, ça use
Trois kilomètres à pied, Ça use les souliers.

Teacher Excusez-moi, Monsieur (or Madame). Pour aller au château, s'il vous plaît ?
Passer-by 3 *(points straight on)* Le château ? Allez tout droit.
Teacher Merci, Monsieur (or Madame). *(Says again to pupils)* On y va !
Pupils C'est loin !

Scene 4

Class *(looking tired out)* Où est le château ?
Pupil 1 On est fatigué !
Pupil 2 C'est loin !
Teacher *(points to castle)* Silence, les enfants ! Voilà le château …
Class *(excited)* C'est le château ! Super !
Teacher *(reads sign on door and puts hands to head in despair)*
Ah non ! Le château est fermé !

5. Vive le temps d'hiver !

Teacher's page

Vocabulary:	Days of the week; dates; weather; likes and dislikes
Functions:	Saying the date; describing the weather; saying what you like/ don't like
Grammar	Il fait/Il y a + weather; j'aime/ je n'aime pas; on form of verb
Characters	4+ (presenter, Santa, one or more reindeer, one or more elves)
Props:	Laptop computer or mock computer screen; flashcards showing different weather and dates (to be held up at the appropriate time)
Costumes:	Santa costume; elf hat(s); reindeer antlers
Sound effects:	Sleigh bells
Set:	Santa's grotto; Christmas decorations, if wanted
Chorus possible:	Yes (elf part can be split; reindeer can speak as chorus)

Notes

- This would be a suitable sketch for a non-religious Christmas show.
- The song *Vive le vent* is a well-known French Christmas song, sung to the tune of Jingle Bells. Learn the song before starting on the play.
- In France, children traditionally receive their presents on Christmas Eve.

Translation

Long live winter-time!

Reindeer and Elf/Elves	Long live the wind (x2) Long live the winter-time wind Which goes off whistling and blowing through the big green Christmas trees. Oh!
Presenter	The North Pole. Monday, the 21st of December.
Santa	Good morning, friends! What's the weather like in France?
Elf	Hmm ... it's hot. It's sunny.
Reindeer	It's hot? Oh dear! I don't like that! We're staying here!
Santa	It's hot ... that's a shame.
Presenter	Tuesday, the 22nd of December.
Santa	Good morning, friends! What's the weather like in France?
Elf	Hmm ... it's windy.
Reindeer	It's windy? Oh dear! I don't like that! We're staying here!
Santa	It's windy ... that's a shame.
Presenter	Wednesday, the 23rd of December.
Santa	Good morning, friends! What's the weather like in France?
Elf	Hmm ... it's not nice. It's raining.
Reindeer	It's raining? Oh dear! I don't like that! We're staying here!
Santa	It's raining ... that's a shame.
Presenter	Thursday, the 24th of December.
Santa	Good morning, friends! What's the weather like in France today?
Elf	It's cold. It's snowing!
Reindeer	It's snowing? Oh yes! Great! I love that!
Santa	It's snowing ... that's perfect. It's Christmas. Let's go!
All	Merry Christmas!
Song as above, adding	Long live the time (x2) Long live wintertime. Snowballs and New Year's Day And a Happy New Year, Granny!

5. Vive le temps d'hiver !

Santa's grotto

Reindeer and Elf/Elves *(singing, to the tune of Jingle Bells):*
>Vive le vent, vive le vent,
>Vive le vent d'hiver
>Qui s'en va sifflant, soufflant
>Dans les grands sapins verts.
>Oh !

Presenter	*(to audience)*	Au Pôle Nord. Lundi, vingt-et-un décembre.
Santa	*(enters)*	Bonjour, mes amis ! Quel temps fait-il en France ?
Elf	*(consults computer)*	Hmm … il fait chaud. Il y a du soleil.
Reindeer	*(unhappy)*	Il fait chaud ? Oh là là ! Je n'aime pas ça ! On reste ici !
Santa	*(leaves, shaking head sadly)*	Il fait chaud … c'est dommage.

Reindeer shake their bells.

Presenter	*(to audience)*	Mardi, vingt-deux décembre.
Santa	*(enters)*	Bonjour, mes amis ! Quel temps fait-il en France ?
Elf	*(consults computer)*	Hmm … il y a du vent.
Reindeer	*(unhappy)*	Il y a du vent ? Oh là là ! Je n'aime pas ça ! On reste ici !
Santa	*(leaves, shaking head sadly)*	Il y a du vent … c'est dommage.

Reindeer shake their bells.

Presenter	*(to audience)*	Mercredi, vingt-trois décembre.
Santa	*(enters)*	Bonjour, mes amis ! Quel temps fait-il en France ?
Elf	*(consults computer)*	Hmm … il fait mauvais. Il pleut.
Reindeer	*(unhappy)*	Il pleut ? Oh là là ! Je n'aime pas ça ! On reste ici !
Santa	*(leaves, shaking head sadly)*	Il pleut … c'est dommage.

Reindeer shake their bells.

Presenter	*(to audience)*	Jeudi, vingt-quatre décembre.
Santa	*(enters)*	Bonjour, mes amis ! Quel temps fait-il en France aujourd'hui ?
Elf	*(consults computer and answers excitedly)*	Il fait froid. Il neige !
Reindeer	*(happy)*	Il neige ? Ah oui ! Super ! J'adore ça !
Santa	*(happy)*	Il neige … c'est parfait. C'est Noël. On y va !
All		Joyeux Noël !

Reindeer shake their bells and they all set off in convoy singing:

All
>Vive le vent, vive le vent,
>Vive le vent d'hiver
>Qui s'en va sifflant, soufflant
>Dans les grands sapins verts.
>Oh !
>
>Vive le temps, vive le temps,
>Vive le temps d'hiver.
>Boules de neige et jour de l'An
>Et Bonne Année, Grand-mère !

6. Qui aime les fantômes ?

Teacher's page

Vocabulary:	Names of family members (*papa, maman, frère*); *j'aime/je déteste*
Functions:	Simple introductions (*c'est mon/ma ...*); likes/dislikes (*adorer, détester*)
Grammar:	Être: *je suis/tu es/elle est/c'est*; possessive adjectives (*mon/ma/mes; ton/ta/tes*)
Characters:	5 (Audrey (girl), Samuel (brother), Guillaume (Ghost), Mum, Dad)
Props:	Pillow and teddy bear for bedroom; table cloth, 4 plates and cutlery for scene at the table; plate full of greens (spinach); exercise book (for history) and pen; TV screen
Costumes:	White sheet for Ghost
Sound effects:	(Optional) spooky ghostly sounds
Set:	Labels to put on desks in different parts of the classroom (*la chambre d'Audrey; la salle à manger; le salon*)
Chorus possible:	Yes (class could join the ghost when he says 'Ouuuuuuuuh !')

Notes

- Get pupils to practise various facial expressions which they will need (eg scared, kind, hungry, surprised, really puzzled, showing dislike, winking).

Translation

Who likes ghosts?

Scene 1
Ghost Ouuuuuuuuh!
Audrey A g-g-g-ghost!
Ghost Yes, I am Guillaume, the friendly ghost.
Audrey He-he-hello, Guillaume! My ... my ... name's Audrey.
Ghost Hello Audrey. I'm hungry! Shall we eat?
Audrey But what about my mum? My dad? My brother?
Ghost I'm invisible, except to you!

Scene 2
Audrey This is my Dad.
Dad Er ... Yes, Audrey, I'm your dad!
Ghost Ouuuuuuuuuuuuuuuh!
Audrey This is my mum.
Mum Er ... Yes, Audrey, I'm your mum!
Ghost Ouuuuuuuuuuuuuuuh!
Audrey This is my brother, Samuel.
Samuel Er ... Yes, Audrey, I'm your brother, Samuel!
Ghost Ouuuuuuuuuuuuuuuh!
Mum Audrey, you are weird, very weird!
Ghost Ha ha ha!

Scene 3
Audrey Oh, spinach! Yuk! I hate that!
Ghost Mmm! I love spinach. Yum-yum!
Audrey OK! Mmm!. Spinach is great!
Mum But, Audrey, you hate spinach!
Audrey No, I love it!
Mum Audrey, you are weird, very weird!
Ghost Ha ha ha!

Scene 4
Audrey Oh no! My history homework! I hate it!
Ghost I love history! Shall I help you?
Audrey Dad, here's my history homework. Great, isn't it?
Dad But, Audrey, you hate history!
Audrey No, no, I love it!
Dad Audrey, you are weird, very weird!
Ghost Ha ha ha!

Scene 5
Audrey It's a film about ghosts. I hate it!
Ghost I love ghosts! Shall we watch the film?
Audrey Ha ha ha! Great film!
Samuel But, Audrey, you hate ghosts!
Audrey No, no, I love them!
Dad, Mum + Samuel Audrey, you are weird, very weird!
Ghost Ouuuuuuuuuuuuuuuh!

© Danièle Bourdais, Sue Finnie and Brilliant Publications Limited

6. Qui aime les fantômes ?

Scene 1 – Audrey's bedroom

Ghost	Ouuuuuuuuh !
Audrey	*(very scared)* Un f-f-f-fantôme !!!!!!!!
Ghost	*(kindly, wanting to shake hands)* Oui ! Je suis Guillaume, le gentil fantôme.
Audrey	*(shaking hands)* Bon … Bonj … Bonjour, Guillaume ! Je … je … je m'appelle Audrey.
Ghost	Bonjour, Audrey ! *(sniffing the air and rubbing his belly)* Oh, j'ai faim. On mange ?
Audrey	Mais … Ma maman ? Mon papa ? Mon frère ?
Ghost	*(leaving bedroom with Audrey)* Je suis invisible, sauf pour toi. *(laughing)* Ha ha ha !

Scene 2 – Around the table in the dining room

Audrey	*(pointing to her dad, whispering)* Là, c'est mon papa.
Dad	*(surprised)* Euh … Oui, Audrey, je suis ton papa !
Ghost	*(waving to Dad, who can't see him)* Ouuuuuuuuuuuuuuuh !
Audrey	*(pointing to her Mum, whispering)* Là, c'est ma maman.
Mum	*(surprised)* Euh … Oui, Audrey, je suis ta maman !
Ghost	*(waving to Mum, who can't see him)* Ouuuuuuuuuuuuuuuh !
Audrey	*(pointing to her brother, whispering)* Là, c'est mon frère, Samuel.
Samuel	*(surprised)* Euh … Oui, Audrey, je suis ton frère, Samuel !
Ghost	*(waving to brother, who can't see him)* Ouuuuuuuuuuuuuuuh !
Mum	*(puzzled)* Audrey, tu es bizarre, très bizarre !
Ghost	*(laughing)* Ha ha ha !

Scene 3

Audrey	*(frowning at her plate)*	Mmm, des épinards ! Beurk ! Je déteste ça !
Ghost	*(eating from Audrey's plate)*	Mmm ! Moi, j'adore les épinards ! Miam-miam !
Audrey	*(looking happy)*	OK ! Mmm ! … Super, les épinards !
Mum	*(suprised)*	Mais, Audrey, tu détestes les épinards !
Audrey	*(showing an empty plate)*	Non, non, j'adore ça !
Mum	*(puzzled)*	Audrey, tu es bizarre, très bizarre !
Ghost	*(laughing)*	Ha ha ha !

Scene 4 – In the lounge, Audrey at a table with exercise book and pen; others watching TV

Audrey	*(scratching her head)*	Oh non ! Mes devoirs d'histoire ! Beurk ! Je déteste ça !
Ghost	*(scribbling in her book)*	Moi, j'adore l'histoire ! Je t'aide ?
Audrey	*(showing Dad her homework)*	Papa ! Voilà mes devoirs d'histoire ! Super, non !
Dad	*(surprised)*	Mais, Audrey, tu détestes l'histoire !
Audrey		Non, non, j'adore ça !
Dad	*(puzzled)*	Audrey, tu es bizarre, très bizarre !
Ghost	*(laughing)*	Ha ha ha !

Scene 5 – watching TV

Audrey	*(watching TV)*	C'est un film de fantômes. Je déteste ça.
Ghost	*(settling in front of TV)*	Moi, j'adore les fantômes ! On regarde le film ?
Audrey	*(laughs)*	Ha ha ha ! Super, le film !
Samuel	*(surprised)*	Mais, Audrey, tu détestes les fantômes !
Audrey	*(winking at Ghost sitting next to her)*	Non, non ! J'adore les fantômes !
Dad, Mum + Samuel *(puzzled)*		Audrey, tu es bizarre, très bizarre !
Ghost + Audrey *(winking at audience)*		Ouuuuuuuuuuuuuuuuh !

7. J'ai du talent !

Teacher's page

Vocabulary:	Musical instruments; opinions
Functions:	Saying your name; asking/saying what instrument you play; giving your opinion
Grammar:	Jouer de + musical instrument; c'est + adjective
Characters:	8+ (presenter, 2 judges, 3 competitors, audience: 2+ pupils/rest of class)
Props:	Microphone for presenter; musical instruments, if possible
Costumes:	None needed, but judges/competitors could wear smart clothes
Sound effects:	Music extracts, if pupils are not playing instruments
Set:	A talent show
Chorus possible:	Yes (the Audience can be composed of any number of children)

Notes

- Pupils should be familiar with the format of TV talent shows. The judges might enjoy adopting the character of current judges. Explain that there are similar shows on French TV.
- Ideally, pupils should play real instruments. You can amend the scripts to fit the instruments (Je joue de la batterie, de la trompette, etc). You could also add more contestants playing different instruments, to extend the play.

Translation

I've got talent!

Presenter Hello and welcome to 'I've got talent!' Here are the judges ...
Judge 1 Hello!
Judge 2 Hello!
Presenter And now, make some noise for Contestant number one!
Contestant 1 Hello, my name is Léo/Léa Leblanc.
Presenter Léo/Léa, do you play a musical instrument?
Contestant 1 Yes, I play the piano.
Presenter Very good, we're listening
Audience Bravo! Again! Excellent! Great! Well played!
Presenter Judge number one?
Judge 1 Super! Well played!
Presenter Judge number two?
Judge 2 Yes, that's great ... Great!
Contestant 1 Thank you. Goodbye.
Presenter And now, make some noise for Contestant number two!
Contestant 2 Hello, my name is Lucas/Lucie Lenoir.
Presenter Lucas/Lucie, do you play a musical instrument?
Contestant 2 Yes, I play the violin.
Presenter Very good, we're listening.
Audience: Rubbish! Boring! Awful!
Presenter Judge number one?
Judge 1 Hmm ... It's boring!
Presenter Judge number two?
Judge 2 No, no, no ... That's awful! It's rubbish!
Contestant 2 Thank you. Goodbye.
Presenter And now, make some noise for Contestant number three!
Contestant 3 Hello, my name is Maxime/Marie Legrand.
Presenter Maxime/Marie, do you play a musical instrument?
Contestant 3 Yes, I play the guitar.
Presenter Very good, we're listening.
Audience: Wonderful! Encore! Well done! Great! Well played!
Presenter Judge number one?
Judge 1 Impressive! That's great!
Presenter Judge number two?
Judge 2 Yes, well done! That's wonderful!
Contestant 3 Thank you. Goodbye.
Presenter So, Audience ... Who is going to win?
Audience Number one ... Number two ... Number three ...
Judge 1 Quiet, please! We have decided. The winner is ...
Judge 2 Number one!
Contestant 1 Thank you, thank you. That's great!
Presenter So, this evening the winner is number one, Léo/Léa Leblanc! That's great! Goodbye and see you next week!

7. J'ai du talent !

A TV talent show stage set. The two judges sit side by side, the presenter stands by them. The Audience are to one side.

Presenter	(to Audience)	Bonjour et bienvenue à « J'ai du talent ! » Voici les juges …
Judge 1	(waves. Audience applauds)	Bonjour !
Judge 2	(waves. Audience applauds)	Bonjour !
Presenter	(indicates Contestant 1)	Et maintenant, faites du bruit pour le candidat numéro un !
Contestant 1	(walks onto stage and bows. Audience applauds)	Bonjour, je m'appelle Léo (or Léa) Leblanc.
Presenter	(to Contestant 1)	Léo (or Léa), tu joues d'un instrument de musique ?
Contestant 1		Oui, je joue du piano.
Presenter		Très bien, on écoute.

Contestant 1 sits at piano and plays a short tune. At the end, Audience applauds and calls out.

Audience		Bravo ! Encore ! Excellent ! Génial ! Bien joué !
Presenter	(turns to Judge 1)	Juge numéro un ?
Judge 1	(smiles)	Super ! Bien joué !
Presenter	(turns to Judge 2)	Juge numéro deux ?
Judge 2	(smiles)	Oui, c'est génial … Génial !
Contestant 1	(happy)	Merci. Au revoir !
Presenter	(indicates Contestant 2)	Et maintenant, faites du bruit pour le candidat numéro deux !
Contestant 2	(walks onto stage and bows. Audience applauds)	Bonjour, je m'appelle Lucas (or Lucie) Lenoir.
Presenter	(to Contestant 2)	Lucas (or Lucie), tu joues d'un instrument de musique ?
Contestant 2		Oui, je joue du violon.
Presenter		Très bien, on écoute.

Contestant 2 plays a short squeaky tune on violin. At the end, feeble applause/some boos.

Audience		Nul! Ennuyeux ! Affreux !
Presenter	(turns to Judge 1)	Juge numéro un ?
Judge 1	(frowns)	Hmm … C'est ennuyeux !
Presenter	(turns to Judge 2)	Juge numéro deux ?
Judge 2	(frowns/shakes head)	Non, non, non … C'est affreux ! C'est nul !
Contestant 2	(sad)	Merci. Au revoir !

Presenter	(indicates Contestant 3) Et maintenant, faites du bruit pour le candidat numéro trois !
Contestant 3	(walks onto stage and bows. Audience applauds) Bonjour, je m'appelle Maxime (or Marie) Legrand.
Presenter	(to Contestant 3) Maxime (or Marie), tu joues d'un instrument de musique ?
Contestant 3	Oui, je joue de la guitare.
Presenter	Très bien, on écoute.

Contestant 3 plays a short tune on guitar. At the end, Audience applauds and calls out.

Audience	Formidable ! Bis ! Bravo ! Génial ! Bien joué !
Presenter	(turns to Judge 1) Juge numéro un ?
Judge 1	(smiles) Impressionnant ! C'est génial !
Presenter	(turns to Judge 2) Juge numéro deux ?
Judge 2	(smiles) Oui, bravo ! C'est formidable !
Contestant 3	(happy) Merci. Au revoir !
Presenter	(to Audience) Alors, le public … Qui va gagner ?
Audience	(each call out a number) Numéro un … numéro deux … numéro trois …
Judge 1	(stands, raises hand) Silence, s'il vous plaît ! Nous avons décidé. Le gagnant, c'est …
Judge 2	(stands) Le numéro un !
Contestant 1	(victorious) Merci ! Merci ! C'est génial !
Presenter	Alors, ce soir, le gagnant, c'est … le numéro un: Léo (or Léa) Leblanc ! C'est génial ! Au revoir et à la semaine prochaine !

Audience applauds.

8. Le lièvre et la tortue

Teacher's page

Vocabulary:	Bonjour/au revoir; Où habites-tu ?; J'habite … ; verbs of movement (avancer, continuer, je suis rapide/lent(e), têtue, stupide, j'ai gagné/j'ai perdu)
Functions:	Asking someone where they live; saying where you live; saying if you are quick/slow; saying you have won/lost
Grammar:	Adverbs (rapidement, lentement; je suis + adjective
Characters:	3 (presenter, hare, tortoise + other non-speaking animal characters, if wanted)
Props:	Number cards 5 and 6 to pin to runners' vests; whistle for presenter; carrots
Costumes:	Masks for the animals; shorts and running vests or tracksuits for the animals
Sound effects:	None
Set:	A marathon race in the countryside
Chorus possible:	Yes (the presenter's part could be divided among several children)

Notes
- This play is based on Aesop's fable, *The Hare and the Tortoise*. You could discuss the moral of the tale with the class.

Translation

8. The hare and the tortoise

Scene 1
Presenter Welcome everyone! Today, it's the animal marathon. Number five is Hare. Hello, Hare. Where do you live?
Hare I live in a hole, in the forest.
Presenter Number six is Tortoise. Hello, Tortoise. Where do you live?
Tortoise I live under a rock, in the desert.
Presenter Three … two … one … Go!
Hare I'm fast … Goodbye, Tortoise!
Tortoise I'm slow … but I'm determined.

Scene 2
Presenter After an hour, Hare is moving forward quickly.
Hare No problem! Ha ha ha!
Presenter Tortoise is moving forward too … but slowly … very slowly …
Tortoise No problem!

Scene 3
Presenter After two hours, where is Hare?
Hare Here I am! I'm eating carrots. Yum-yum!
Presenter Where is Tortoise?
Tortoise Here I am! I'm moving forward … slowly, slowly. No problem!

Scene 4
Presenter After three hours, where is Hare?
Hare I'm going to have a little sleep … I've got time. No problem!
Presenter Where is Tortoise?
Tortoise I'm determined, I'm going to keep going. No problem!

Scene 5
Presenter After four hours, Tortoise overtakes Hare.
Tortoise I'm determined, I'm keeping on going. No problem!

Scene 6
Presenter After ten hours, Tortoise arrives at the finishing line.
Tortoise I've won! I've won! I'm slow, but I'm determined!
Presenter Well done, Tortoise!
Hare Oh no! I've lost! I'm quick but I'm stupid!

8. Le lièvre et la tortue

Scene 1

Presenter *(to audience)* Bienvenue à tous ! Aujourd'hui, c'est le marathon des animaux. Le numéro cinq, c'est Lièvre. *(to Hare)* Bonjour, Lièvre. Où habites-tu ?

Hare J'habite dans un trou, dans la forêt.

Presenter *(to Tortoise)* Le numéro six, c'est Tortue. Bonjour, Tortue. Où habites-tu ?

Tortoise J'habite sous un rocher, dans le désert.

Presenter *(raises starting whistle)* Trois … deux … un ! Partez ! *(blows whistle)*

Hare *(sets off, running)* Je suis rapide … Au revoir, Tortue !

Tortoise *(sets off, plodding)* Je suis lente … mais je suis têtue.

Scene 2

Presenter *(to audience)* Après une heure, Lièvre avance rapidement.

Hare *(runs across stage)* Pas de problème ! Hi hi hi !

Presenter Tortue aussi avance … mais lentement … très lentement …

Tortoise *(plods slowly across stage)* Pas de problème !

Scene 3

Presenter *(to audience)* Après deux heures, où est Lièvre ?

Hare *(lounging eating carrots)* Me voilà ! Je mange des carottes. Miam-miam !

Presenter Où est Tortue ?

Tortoise *(still plodding on)* Me voilà ! J'avance … lentement, lentement. Pas de problème !

Scene 4

Presenter *(to audience)* Après trois heures, où est Lièvre ?

Hare *(yawns and lies down to sleep)* Je vais dormir un peu … J'ai le temps. Pas de problème !

Presenter Où est Tortue ?

Tortoise *(plods on)* Je suis têtue, je continue. Pas de problème !

Scene 5

Presenter Après quatre heures, Tortue dépasse Lièvre.
(Hare lying on the ground, snoring)

Tortoise *(plods slowly past the sleeping Hare)* Je suis têtue, je continue. Pas de problème !

Scene 6

Presenter Après dix heures, Tortue arrive à la ligne d'arrivée.

Tortoise *(plods happily across the finishing line)* J'ai gagné ! J'ai gagné ! *(winks at audience)* Je suis lente mais je suis têtue !

Presenter *(clapping)* Bravo, Tortue !

Hare *(rushes up behind, annoyed at losing)* Ah non ! J'ai perdu ! Je suis rapide mais je suis stupide !

9. Le cheval du désert

Teacher's page

Vocabulary: Animals (*le cheval, la girafe, le chameau, l'autruche, le dromadaire*); parts of the body (*le cou, les pattes, le dos*); time words (*le matin, le midi, le soir*)

Functions: Greetings (*bonjour, ça va ?*, etc); saying how you feel (*ça va/ça ne va pas, j'ai faim/soif/froid*); saying thanks (*merci, c'est sympa*)

Grammar: Phrases with avoir (*j'ai faim/soif/froid*); imperatives (*mange, marche, mets*); verb pouvoir (*je ne peux pas*); simple negative (*je n'ai pas de …*)

Characters: 5 (narrator, a horse, a giraffe, a camel, an ostrich)

Props: A branch with leaves; drawings on cardboard of a dromedary's neck, legs and hump; an enlarged picture of a dromedary; pins or Blu-tack®

Costumes: Home-made masks (horse, giraffe, camel, ostrich)

Sound effects: (Optional) African drumming

Set: Anything to suggest nature

Chorus possible: Greek chorus for narrator parts

Notes

- This play is based on a traditional North African tale. Point out that many people in countries in North Africa – like Algeria, Morocco and Tunisia – are French-speaking.
- The play touches on habitats (desert, dry and cold at night) and how animals adapt to their environment, offering cross-curricular links with topic work on habitats.
- The play also offers an opportunity to work on sound-spelling links (mostly rhyming words containing the sounds 'a' and 'oi').

Translation

The desert horse

Scene 1

Narrator Here is a little horse. He lives in the desert. He's not happy. He doesn't like the desert.
Giraffe Hello Horse, are you all right?
Horse Hello, Giraffe. No, I'm not.
Giraffe What's the matter?
Horse I'm hungry in the morning!
Giraffe Eat leaves, like I do!
Horse I don't have a long neck. I can't!
Giraffe Here is a long neck.
Horse Thanks Giraffe, it's kind of you.

Scene 2

Camel Hello, Horse, are you all right?
Horse Hello, Camel. No, I'm not.
Camel What's the matter?
Horse I'm thirsty at midday!
Camel Use a hump on your back, like I do!
Horse I don't have a hump. I can't!
Camel Here is a hump.
Horse Thanks, Camel, it's kind of you!

Scene 3

Ostrich Hello, Horse. Are you all right?
Horse Hello, Ostrich. No, I'm not.
Ostrich What's the matter?
Horse I'm cold at night!
Ostrich Walk fast, like I do!
Horse I don't have long legs. I can't!
Ostrich Here are long legs.
Horse Thanks, Ostrich, it's kind of you!

Scene 4

Horse I have a long neck, a hump and long legs. I'm not hungry, I'm not thirsty, I'm not cold anymore! Great!
I love the desert!
Narrator A horse with a long neck, a hump and long legs …
It's a desert horse, it's a dromedary!

© Danièle Bourdais, Sue Finnie and Brilliant Publications Limited

9. Le cheval du désert

Scene 1

Narrator (*pointing at horse, ambling and looking miserable*) Voici un petit cheval. Il habite dans le désert. Ça ne va pas. Il n'aime pas le désert.

Giraffe Bonjour, Cheval ! Ça va ?

Horse (*miserable*) Bonjour, Girafe ! Non, ça ne va pas.

Giraffe Et pourquoi ?

Horse J'ai faim le matin !

Giraffe (*pointing to high branch with leaves*) Mange des feuilles, comme moi !

Horse (*trying to get at leaves*) Je n'ai pas de long cou. Je ne peux pas !

Giraffe (*handing out a long neck*) Tiens, un long cou, voilà.

Horse (*happy*) Merci, Girafe, c'est sympa ! (*walks on and pins picture of long neck on board*)

Scene 2

Camel Bonjour, Cheval ! Ça va ?

Horse (*miserable*) Bonjour, Chameau ! Non, ça ne va pas.

Camel Et pourquoi ?

Horse J'ai soif le midi !

Camel Mets une bosse sur ton dos, comme moi !

Horse Je n'ai pas de bosse, je ne peux pas !

Camel (*handing out a hump*) Tiens, une bosse, voilà.

Horse (*happy*) Merci, Chameau, c'est sympa ! (*walks on and pins picture of hump on board*)

Scene 3

Ostrich Bonjour, Cheval ! Ça va ?

Horse (*miserable*) Bonjour, Autruche ! Non, ça ne va pas.

Ostrich Et pourquoi ?

Horse J'ai froid le soir !

Ostrich (*running very fast*) Marche vite, comme moi !

Horse (*trying to run fast but can't*) Je n'ai pas de longues pattes. Je ne peux pas !

Ostrich (*handing out 4 long legs*) Tiens, des longues pattes, voilà.

Horse (*happy*) Merci, Autruche, c'est sympa ! (*walks on and pins picture of legs on board*)

Scene 4

Horse (*pointing to parts of body on the board*)
J'ai un long cou, une bosse et des longues pattes ... (*pins his own horse face mask on board*)
Je n'ai plus faim, je n'ai plus soif, je n'ai plus froid ! Super !
J'aime bien le désert ! (*runs out happily*)

Narrator (*pointing to parts of body*)
Un cheval avec un long cou, une bosse et des longues pattes ...
C'est un cheval du désert ... (*producing photo of dromedary*) C'est un dromadaire !

10. La ronde des mois

Teacher's page

Vocabulary:	Months of the year (*janvier, février,* etc); seasons (*printemps, été, automne, hiver*); festivals (*galette des Rois, Chandeleur, fête nationale, Noël*)	**Costumes:**	None
		Sound effects:	None
		Set:	None
		Chorus possible:	Yes (whole-class repetition of the names of the months and final part)
Functions:	Say what you have done (*j'ai mangé, j'ai vu, j'ai dit, j'ai dansé, j'ai mis, j'ai fait*)		
Grammar:	Perfect tense with avoir (*j'ai mangé, j'ai vu,* etc)		
Characters:	2–12 (either done in pairs – with pupils alternating the months – or with each month represented by a different person)		
Props:	Round flat cake + golden paper crown; cardboard pancake + frying pan; picture of rainbow; Easter egg; picture of lily of the valley bouquet; school bag + sun glasses; French flag; bucket and spade; scarf; witches' hat + toy rat (or picture); real or hand-painted multi-coloured leaves; wrapped Christmas present		

Notes

- This 'playlet' (or tableau) is suitable for assemblies; it presents the various festivals and celebrations of the French year: Epiphany and the Three Kings (6th January), pancake making on Candlemas (2nd February), Easter Eggs (March or April), May Day and its traditional good luck flower, end of school (late June), National Day (14th July), back to school (early September), Halloween (31st October), Christmas (December).
- This play offers cross-curricular work on the themes of 'festivals' and 'seasons'.

Translation

All year round

January	I've eaten the Epiphany cake. I am January. What about you?
February	I've eaten pancakes on Shrove Tuesday. I am February. What about you?
March	I've seen the Spring rainbow. I am March. What about you?
April	I've eaten some chocolate eggs. I am April. What about you?
May	I've made a bouquet of lily of the valley. I am May. What about you?
June	I've said 'Goodbye, school!', 'Hello Summer!' I am June. What about you?
July	I've danced at the Bastille Day ball. I am July. What about you?
August	I've made a beautiful sandcastle. I am August. What about you?
September	I've put on my autumn clothes for school. I am September. What about you?
October	I've seen ghosts, witches and rats. I am October. What about you?
November	I've seen leaves of different colours. I am November. What about you?
December	I've said 'Hello, winter!' and 'Merry Christmas!' I am December. That's it!
All	January, February, March, April, May, June, July, August, September, October, November, December. We are the months of the year. A Happy New Year in French, a Happy New Year for all!

© Danièle Bourdais, Sue Finnie and Brilliant Publications Limited

10. La ronde des mois

January (holding a round flat cake and putting a golden paper crown on head)
J'ai mangé la galette des Rois ! Je suis Janvier. Et toi ?

February (holding a frying pan and tossing a pancake)
J'ai mangé les crêpes de la Chandeleur ! Je suis Février. Et toi ?

March (holding a painted rainbow in the air and looking up at it)
J'ai vu l'arc-en-ciel du printemps ! Je suis Mars. Et toi ?

April (holding Easter egg)
J'ai mangé des œufs en chocolat ! Je suis Avril. Et toi ?

May (holding lily of the valley)
J'ai fait un bouquet de muguet ! Je suis Mai. Et toi ?

June (throwing down school bag and putting on sun glasses)
J'ai dit « Au revoir, école », « Bonjour, été » ! Je suis Juin ! Et toi ?

July (dancing while waving a French flag)
J'ai dansé au bal de la fête nationale ! Je suis Juillet. Et toi ?

August (playing with bucket and spade)
J'ai fait un beau château de sable ! Je suis Août ! Et toi ?

September (putting on a scarf and picking up school bag)
J'ai mis mes habits d'automne et de rentrée. Je suis Septembre. Et toi ?

October (wearing a witches' hat and holding toy rat)
J'ai vu des fantômes, des sorcières et des rats ! Je suis Octobre. Et toi ?

November (throwing multi-coloured leaves)
J'ai vu des feuilles de toutes les couleurs ! Je suis Novembre. Et toi ?

December (holding Christmas present)
J'ai dit « Bonjour, l'hiver » et « Joyeux Noël ! » Je suis Décembre. Et voilà !

All (chanting)
Janvier, février, mars, avril, mai, juin, juillet, août, septembre, octobre, novembre, décembre !
Nous sommes les mois de l'année. Bonne année en français ! Bonne année à tous !

11. Jacques et le haricot magique

Teacher's page

Vocabulary:	Plant growing (*une graine, une tige, des feuilles, pousser*; adjectives (*pauvre, petite, maigre, magique, méchant, riche, fatigué*)
Functions:	Saying what you have (*j'ai*); saying what you see (*je vois …*); asking what something is (*C'est quoi ?*)
Grammar:	Immediate future (*tu vas vendre, tu vas être, je vais planter, je vais monter, je vais prendre, je vais dormir, je vais être*)
Characters:	7 (Jack, Mum, Blanchette, old man, man and woman in market, Giant)
Props:	Bean seed; bean stalk painted on roll of paper; chair and table or a ladder (for Jack to climb on, hidden behind the beanstalk); baskets for people in market; a treasure chest
Costumes:	Cow mask and lead for Blanchette; walking stick for old man
Sound effects:	(Optional) magical bell sound
Set:	2 tables (one for ogre, another for Jack to climb on)
Chorus possible:	None

Notes

- Pupils will be familiar with the traditional British tale on which this play is based. It is also studied in French primary schools.
- Cross-curricular links are possible with the theme of 'plants and growing'.

Translation

Jack and the beanstalk

Scene 1

Old man	Once upon a time, there was a boy. He was poor, very poor …
Jack	Mum! I'm hungry!
Blanchette	Moo! Moo!
Mum	I'm sorry, Jack, there is nothing.
Jack	Oh dear! I'm hungry!
Blanchette	Moo! Moo!
Mum	Tomorrow, you'll go and sell the cow at the market.
Jack	Oh, poor Blanchette!
Blanchette	Moo! Moo!

Scene 2

Jack	Hello, Sir. Do you want to buy my cow?
Blanchette	Moo! Moo!
Man	No! She's too small.
Jack	Hello, Madam. Do you want to buy my cow?
Blanchette	Moo! Moo!
Woman	No! She's too thin.
Old man	Jacques! Jacques! Here is a seed in exchange for your cow.
Jack	A seed in exchange for my cow?
Old man	It's a magic bean! Tomorrow, you will be rich!
Jack	Bye, Blanchette!
Blanchette	Moo! Moo!

Scene 3

Jack	Mum, I've got a seed in exchange for the cow!
Mum	A seed?!
Jack	It's a magic bean!
Mum	Impossible! Impossible! Grrrr …
Jack	I'm going to plant the seed. Mum, look! The stalk is growing! The leaves are growing!
Mum	A magic bean? Impossible! Impossible … !

Scene 4

Jack	I'm going to climb up.
Mum	Be careful, Jacques! It's very high!
Jack	I can see a castle … I can see a treasure! Oops! I can see a Giant!
Giant	I'm a Giant. I am nasty. I find little children tasty (literally: I'm going to eat a child) Ahhh … I'm tired, I'm going to sleep … zzz zzz!
Jack	Ha ha! … I'll take the treasure. I'll be rich!
Giant	Aaaaah! The treasure! Where is the treasure? What is it? A beanstalk? What is it? A child? Grrrrrrrrrrrrrr!
Jack	Goodbye, Giant! Mum! I have the treasure! Thank you, magic bean!
Blanchette	Moo! Moo! Moo! Moo!
Jack + Mum	Hello, Blanchette!
Old man	The end!

11. Jacques et le haricot magique

Scene 1 – Jacques, his mother and their cow are at home

Old man *(at the side of the stage)* Il était une fois un garçon pauvre, très pauvre …

Jack *(starving)* Maman ! J'ai faim !

Blanchette, the cow *(starving)* Meuh ! Meuh !

Mum *(looking sorry)* Désolée, Jacques. Il n'y a rien.

Jack Oh là là ! J'ai faim !

Blanchette Meuh ! Meuh !

Mum *(pointing to cow)* Demain, tu vas vendre la vache au marché.

Jack *(sad)* Oh ! Pauvre Blanchette !

Blanchette *(sad)* Meuh ! Meuh !

Scene 2 – In the market place

Jack *(holding cow on a lead, showing her to a man)* Bonjour, monsieur. Vous achetez ma vache ?

Blanchette Meuh ! Meuh !

Man *(frowning)* Non ! Elle est trop petite !

Jack *(showing cow to a woman)* Bonjour, madame. Vous achetez ma vache ?

Blanchette Meuh ! Meuh !

Woman *(frowning)* Non ! Elle est trop maigre !

Old man *(taps Jacques on the shoulder)* Jacques ! Jacques ! *(gives him a bean)* Voilà une graine pour ta vache.

Jack *(surprised)* Une graine pour ma vache ?

Old man C'est un haricot magique, Jacques. Demain, tu vas être riche !

Jack *(waving sadly to cow)* Au revoir, Blanchette !

Blanchette *(being led away by mysterious old man)* Meuh ! Meuh !

Scene 3 – In Jacques' home

Jack *(excited)* Maman, j'ai une graine pour la vache !

Mum *(astonished)* Une graine ?

Jack C'est un haricot magique !

Mum *(really angry)* Impossible ! Impossible ! Grrrr …

Jack *(planting the seed)* Je vais planter la graine. *(Excited, pointing to beanstalk, which is growing)* Maman, regarde ! La tige pousse ! Les feuilles poussent !

Mum *(can't believe it)* Un haricot magique ? Impossible ! Impossible … !

Scene 4

Jack	*(climbing up the beanstalk)*	Je vais monter.
Mum	*(looking up)*	Attention, Jacques ! C'est très haut !
Jack	*(to his Mum, looking down from the top of the beanstalk)*	Je vois un château … Je vois un trésor !
	(Giant is lying down – stirs in his sleep)	Oups ! Je vois un ogre !!!
Ogre	*(in his sleep)*	Je suis un ogre, je suis méchant. Je vais manger un petit enfant !
	(yawns)	Ahhh … Je suis fatigué. Je vais dormir … *(settling back to sleep and snoring)* ronron ronron …
Jack		Ha ha ! … Je vais prendre le trésor ! Je vais être riche !
	(Jacques steals the treasure chest – Giant wakes up)	
Ogre	*(stretching)*	Aaaaah ! *(shocked)* Le trésor ! Où est le trésor ?
	(seeing the beanstalk)	C'est quoi ? Un haricot ?!
	(seeing Jacques getting away)	C'est quoi ? Un enfant ?!
	(very angry)	Grrrrrrrrrrrrrrr !
Jack	*(waving cheekily)*	Au revoir, Ogre ! *(climbs down)* Maman ! J'ai le trésor ! Merci, haricot magique !
Blanchette	*(led by old man, jumping with joy when seeing Jack and his mum)*	Meuh ! Meuh ! Meuh !
Jack + Mum	*(happy)*	Bonjour, Blanchette !
Old man	*(peeping from the side of the stage and winking)*	Fin !

12. Vive la Révolution !

Teacher's page

Vocabulary:	Relating to the French Revolution (*roi, reine, prison, château, guillotine, monarchie, république*)
Functions:	Description of self (*je suis, j'ai*); act opinion phrases (*ce n'est pas juste, à bas, vive !*)
Grammar:	Phrases with avoir (*j'ai faim, j'ai peur, je n'ai pas de …*)
Characters:	6 or 7+ (narrator, farmer, labourer, Louis XVI, Marie-Antoinette, guard/judge + 'crowd')
Props:	Banners with dates: 1789, 14 juillet 1789, 1792 and 1793; sticks for poor people; guard's sword; hammer for judge; guillotine made of cardboard; French flag
Costumes:	Poor farmer and poor labourer's outfits; 2 colourful gowns and 2 crowns for King and Queen; 1 hat (guard);1 black gown (for judge); blue/red/white rosettes for crowd
Sound effects:	Background music. Ça ira song; gunshots; guillotine sound
Set:	Scene 2: image of gates of Versailles and image of Bastille; Scenes 3 + 4: a desk representing the court
Chorus possible:	Several narrators; crowd of citizens

Notes
- This play is an introduction to why and how the French Revolution began in 1789 (poverty and injustice); storming of the Bastille on July 14; King and Queen removed from Versailles then brought to trial in 1792, and executed in 1793)
- Ça ira!, is a famous revolutionary song.
- Possible cross-curricular links with history.

Translation

12. Long live the Revolution!

Scene 1 (banner: 1789)
Narrator France is poor, France is hungry. But the King is rich, the Queen is rich. It's not fair.
Farmer I'm a peasant! I'm poor! I'm hungry!
Labourer I'm a worker! I'm poor! I'm hungry!
+ Crowd I'm poor! I'm hungry!
Farmer It's King Louis XVI. He's rich!
Labourer Please, your Majesty, give us some bread!
Farmer + Crowd Please! (x2)
King I don't have any bread for you! Leave me alone!
Labourer It's Queen Marie-Antoinette! She's rich!
Farmer Please your Majesty, give us some bread!
Labourer + Crowd Please! (x2)
Queen I don't have any bread for you! Leave me alone!
Farmer It's not fair! Down with the King!
Labourer It's not fair! Down with the Queen!
+ Crowd Long live the Revolution!
Farmer, Labourer + Crowd
All will be fine, will be fine, will be fine,
The Aristocrats will hang from streetlights
All will be fine, will be fine, will be fine,
The Aristocrats, we'll hang them all!

Scene 2 (banner: 14th July 1798)
Narrator In Paris, people don't like the King. People don't like the Bastille, the King's prison.
Farmer That's the Bastille, the King's prison!
Labourer Down with the Bastille! Down with the King!
Guard This is the Bastille, the King's prison! Go away! Go away!
Labourer It's a Revolution!
Farmer Long live the Revolution!
Crowd Long live the Revolution!
Guard A revolution? Aaaah! I'm scared!
Farmer, Labourer + Crowd All will be fine, will be fine etc.

Scene 3 (banner: 1792)
Narrator In France, people no longer want a King or a Queen.
Judge Louis, you're no longer King. You're going to live in prison.
King No way! I live in a chateau, in Versailles!
Judge Marie-Antoinette, you're no longer Queen. You're going to live in prison.
Queen No way! I live in a chateau, in Versailles!
Crowd Monarchy is finished! Long live the Republic!
All will be fine, will be fine etc.

Scene 4 (banner: 1794)
Narrator The King and the Queen are sentenced to death.
Judge Louis, you are an enemy of the Republic. To the guillotine!
King What? No, have mercy!
Judge Marie-Antoinette, you are an enemy of the Republic. To the guillotine!
Queen What? No, have mercy!
Crowd Long live the Revolution! Liberty, equality, fraternity! Long live France!
All will be fine, will be fine, will be fine, etc

12. Vive la Révolution !

Scene 1   (on banner: 1789)

Narrator   *(holding banner)*   La France est pauvre, la France a faim. Mais le roi est riche, et la reine est riche ! Ce n'est pas juste.

Farmer   *(despondent)*   Je suis paysan, je suis pauvre ! J'ai faim !

Labourer   *(despondent)*   Je suis ouvrier, je suis pauvre ! J'ai faim !

+ Crowd   Je suis pauvre ! J'ai faim !

Farmer   *(pointing to King)*   C'est le roi Louis Seize ! Il est riche !

Labourer   *(kneeling in front of King)*   Votre Majesté, du pain, s'il vous plaît !

Farmer   *(kneeling in front of King)*   S'il vous plaît !

+ Crowd   S'il vous plaît !

King   *(dismissing them)*   Je n'ai pas de pain pour vous ! Laissez-moi !

Labourer   *(pointing to Queen)*   C'est la reine Marie-Antoinette ! Elle est riche !

Farmer   *(kneeling in front of Queen)*   Votre Majesté, du pain, s'il vous plaît !

Labourer   *(kneeling in front of Queen)*   S'il vous plaît !

+ Crowd   S'il vous plaît !

Queen   *(dismissing them)*   Je n'ai pas de pain pour vous ! Laissez-moi !

Farmer   *(outraged)*   Ce n'est pas juste ! À bas le roi !

Labourer   *(outraged)*   Ce n'est pas juste ! À bas la reine !

+ Crowd   *(up in arms)*   Vive la Révolution !

Farmer, **Labourer + Crowd** *(singing and marching)*

>Ah ça ira, ça ira, ça ira,
>Les aristocrates à la lanterne
>Ah ça ira, ça ira, ça ira,
>Les aristocrates, on les pendra !

Scene 2   (on banner: 14 juillet 1789)

Narrator   *(holding banner)*   À Paris, on n'aime pas le roi. On n'aime pas la Bastille, la prison du roi.

Farmer   *(pointing and marching towards the Bastille)*   C'est la Bastille, la prison du roi.

Labourer   *(raising stick, marching)*   À bas la Bastille ! À bas le roi ! *(both stop in front of Guard)*

Guard   *(blocking entrance to the prison)*   Ici, c'est la Bastille, la prison du roi. Partez ! Partez !

Labourer   *(raising stick, marching)*   C'est la Révolution !

Farmer   *(waving to Crowd)*   Vive la Révolution !

Crowd   *(marching forward)*   Vive la Révolution !

Guard   *(afraid)*   La Révolution ? Aaaah !!! J'ai peur !

Farmer, **Labourer + Crowd**   La Bastille, c'est fini ! Vive la Révolution !

Crowd   *(singing)*   Ah ça ira, ça ira, ça ira, etc

Scene 3 (on banner: 1792)

Narrator (*holding banner*)   En France, on ne veut plus de roi ; on ne veut plus de reine.

Judge (*hammering on table*)   Louis, tu n'es plus roi. Tu vas habiter en prison !

King (*angry*)   Ah non ! J'habite dans un château, à Versailles !

Judge (*hammering on table*)   Marie-Antoinette, tu n'es plus reine. Tu vas habiter en prison !

Queen (*angry*)   Ah non ! J'habite dans un château, à Versailles !

Crowd (*cheering*)   La Monarchie, c'est fini ! Vive la République !

Crowd (*singing*)   Ah ça ira, ça ira, ça ira, etc

Scene 4 (Narrator holding banner, on banner: 1794)

Narrator   Le roi est condamné à mort. La reine est condamnée à mort.

Judge (*hammering on table*)   Louis, tu es ennemi de la République. À la guillotine !

King (*pleading*)   Quoi ? Non, non, pitié !

(*King is led to the guillotine by Farmer and Labourer – Crowd cheers*)

Judge (*hammering on table*)   Marie-Antoinette, tu es ennemie de la République. À la guillotine !

Queen (*pleading*)   Quoi ? Non, non, pitié !

(*Queen is led to the guillotine by Farmer and Labourer – Crowd cheers*)

Crowd   Vive la Révolution ! Vive la République ! Liberté, égalité, fraternité ! Vive la France !

Crowd (*marching and singing*)   Ah ça ira, ça ira, ça ira, etc.

Au café

Activity Sheet

a) Listen to the play and then copy these sentences into the right bubble.
b) Listen again to check.

> Merci.

> Je n'ai pas 9 euros, j'ai 5 euros.

> Oui, madame. Il y a un problème ?

> Je voudrais une pizza, s'il vous plaît.

1

2

3

4

c) On the back of the sheet, draw a picture to go with these bubbles.

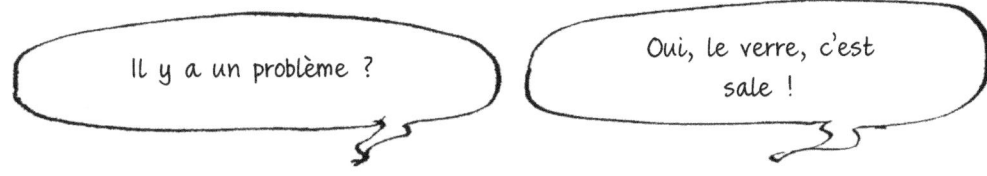

> Il y a un problème ?

> Oui, le verre, c'est sale !

© Danièle Bourdais, Sue Finnie and Brilliant Publications Limited

Bobo le robot

a) Who says it – the inventors or the robots? Copy the sentences into the correct column.

b) Listen to the play to check.

J'ai inventé un robot !	Je suis un robot.	Je m'appelle Toto.
Écoute !	Je regarde.	Je m'assieds !
Génial, non ?	Ça suffit !	Je marche.

Les inventeurs

Les robots

c) Can you add any more phrases to the lists?

Je veux un bonbon !

Activity Sheet

a) Listen to the play and point to each sentence as you hear it.

b) Make up another scene for the play! Think of a different item to ask for and write its name on the lines below.

Example: Je veux <u>une pizza</u> !

c) Cut out the sentences. Mix them up, then rearrange them in the right order.

Je veux _____ !

Non! On dit: « Je voudrais _____ , s'il te plaît. »

Je voudrais _____ , s'il te plaît.

Tiens, _____ .

On dit: « Merci. » … Oh là là, les enfants !

© Danièle Bourdais, Sue Finnie and Brilliant Publications Limited

Un kilomètre à pied

a) Work with a partner.

b) Rearrange the words in the triangles and write sentences to retell the story.

1. les écoutez enfants !
2. on une fait excursion. aujourd'hui
3. au pour aller château s'il vous plaît ?
4. à allez droite.
5. à gauche. allez
6. tout droit. allez
7. on fatigué ! est
8. le voilà château.
9. fermé ! Ah non ! Le est château

Example =
Écoutez, les enfants !

_____

_____

_____

_____

_____

_____

_____

_____

c) Now listen to the play to check your sentences.

d) Can you write the English version of the 10 sentences on the back of this sheet?

Vive le temps d'hiver ! *Activity Sheet*

a) Draw a picture to illustrate each of the weather phrases.

b) Listen to the play and point to the picture when you hear the weather phrase.

c) Practise saying what the weather is like. With a partner, take turns to throw a dice. The number you throw is the number of the picture you describe. Who can be first to say all six phrases?

1 Il y a du soleil.

2 Il pleut.

3 Il y a du vent.

4 Il neige.

5 Il fait chaud.

6 Il fait froid.

Qui aime les fantômes ?

Activity Sheet

a) Cut out the phrases. Place the French ones on your desk. Pick them up as you hear them mentioned in the play.

b) Speed game: match each French phrase with the English phrase.

c) In pairs, play a game of snap with two sets of the cards.

Example: snap when A puts down *Je déteste ça* and B puts down *Je déteste ça* or *I hate it*.

Je déteste ça !	J'adore les épinards !	I'm invisible.
J'adore ça !	J'ai faim.	I hate it!
Là, c'est mon frère.	Je suis invisible.	Let's eat!
On mange ?	I'm hungry.	Let's watch the film.
On regarde le film ?	This is my brother.	It's a film about ghosts.
C'est un film de fantômes.	I love spinach.	I love it!

J'ai du talent !

a) Are these comments from the judges and the audience positive or negative? Listen to the play to help you decide. Then colour the bubbles:

positive = yellow   negative = red

1 Bravo !

2 Bien joué !

3 Nul !

4 Génial !

5 Ennuyeux !

6 Formidable !

7 Affreux !

8 Impressionnant !

b) Choose a word from the box to write under each bubble to show its meaning.

| Impressive! Well done! Awful! Well played! Wonderful! Boring! Rubbish! Great! |

Le lièvre et la tortue

a) Write the missing words in the gaps.

| désert | forêt | lentement | mange | marathon | Où | problème | rapide |

b) Then listen to check.

Presenter Bienvenue à tous !

Aujourd'hui, c'est le _____ des animaux.

Le numéro cinq, c'est Lièvre. Bonjour, Lièvre.

_____ habites-tu ?

Hare J'habite dans un trou, dans la _____

Presenter Le numéro six, c'est Tortue. Bonjour, Tortue.

Où habites-tu ?

Tortoise J'habite sous un rocher, dans le _____

Presenter Trois … deux … un! Partez !

Hare Je suis _____ … au revoir, Tortue !

Tortoise Je suis lente … mais je suis têtue.

Presenter Après une heure, Lièvre avance rapidement.

Hare Pas de problème ! Hi hi hi !

Presenter Tortue aussi avance … mais _____ … très lentement.

Tortoise Pas de problème !

Presenter Après deux heures, où est Lièvre ?

Hare Me voilà ! Je _____ des carottes.

Miam, miam !

Presenter Où est Tortue ?

Tortoise Me voilà ! J'avance … lentement, lentement.

Pas de _____ !

44 © Danièle Bourdais, Sue Finnie and Brilliant Publications Limited

Le cheval du désert

a) Look at the sheet and point to the French phrases as you hear them mentioned in the play.

b) Cut out the dominoes and mix them up. In pairs, play dominoes and re-order the scene.

c) Make your own domino set for the other scenes.

Example:

| No, I'm not ok. | Et pourquoi ? | What's the matter | J'ai soif le midi. |

Dominoes:

| Hello, Horse. Are you all right? | Bonjour, Girafe. Non, ça ne va pas. |

| Bonjour, Cheval. Ça va ? |

| Hello, Giraffe. No, I'm not OK. | Et pourquoi ? |

| What's the matter? | J'ai faim le matin ! |

| I'm hungry in the morning. | Mange des feuilles, comme moi ! |

| Eat leaves, like I do! | Je n'ai pas de long cou. Je ne peux pas. |

| I don't have a long neck. I can't! | Tiens, un long cou, voilà. |

| Here is a long neck. | Merci, Girafe, c'est sympa. |

| Thanks Giraffe, it's kind of you. |

© Danièle Bourdais, Sue Finnie and Brilliant Publications Limited

45

La ronde des mois

Activity Sheet

a) Cut out the sentences and mix them up. Re-order them as you hear the French phrases mentioned.

b) In pairs: divide up the sentences. A reads one, B says the name of the month.

Example: A : J'ai mangé la galette des rois !   B: Janvier !

c) In pairs, re-order all the sentences from memory. Which pair is the quickest?

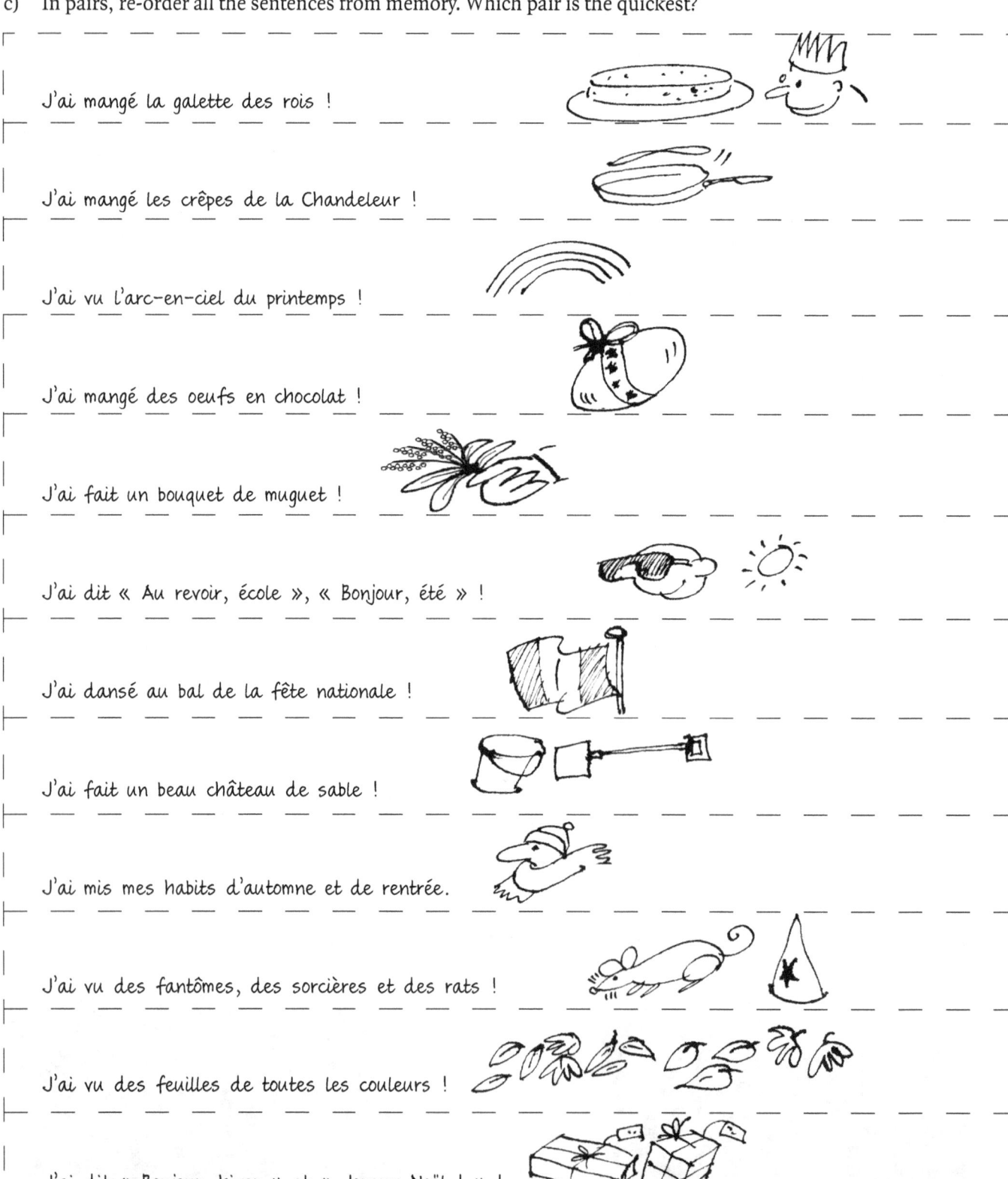

J'ai mangé la galette des rois !

J'ai mangé les crêpes de la Chandeleur !

J'ai vu l'arc-en-ciel du printemps !

J'ai mangé des oeufs en chocolat !

J'ai fait un bouquet de muguet !

J'ai dit « Au revoir, école », « Bonjour, été » !

J'ai dansé au bal de la fête nationale !

J'ai fait un beau château de sable !

J'ai mis mes habits d'automne et de rentrée.

J'ai vu des fantômes, des sorcières et des rats !

J'ai vu des feuilles de toutes les couleurs !

J'ai dit « Bonjour, hiver » et « Joyeux Noël ! » !

46 © Danièle Bourdais, Sue Finnie and Brilliant Publications Limited

Jacques et le haricot magique

Activity Sheet

a) Point to the French sentences when you hear them in the play.

b) Write the English phrase under each French sentence, under the dotted line.

c) Cut out the jigsaw pieces. In pairs, reassemble the jigsaw by matching the French and the English.

d) Make your own jigsaw with other phrases from the play!

Example: J'ai faim/I'm hungry.

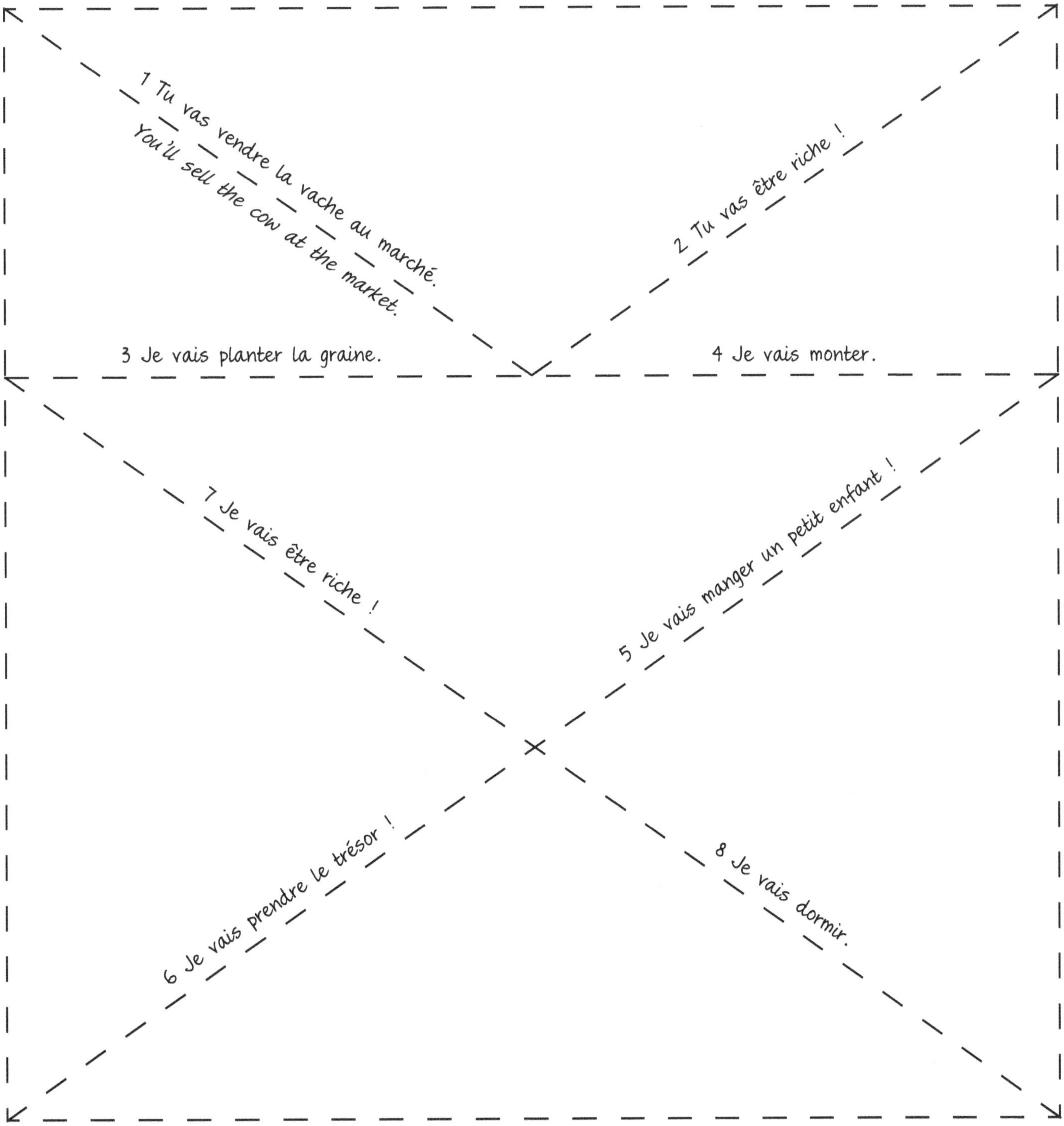

1 Tu vas vendre la vache au marché.
You'll sell the cow at the market.

2 Tu vas être riche !

3 Je vais planter la graine.

4 Je vais monter.

5 Je vais manger un petit enfant !

6 Je vais prendre le trésor !

7 Je vais être riche !

8 Je vais dormir.

Vive la Révolution !

a) Look at the pictures and listen to the play. Discuss what is happening.

b) In pairs: cut out the pictures. Mix them up and re-order them.

c) Fold and hide the text. How well do you remember it?

d) Finally, use the pictures to help you prepare your performance.

Je suis pauvre ! J'ai faim !

Je n'ai pas de pain pour vous ! Laissez-moi !

À bas la Bastille ! À bas le roi !
Vive la Révolution !

Louis, tu n'es plus roi. Tu vas habiter en prison !

Marie-Antoinette, tu es ennemie de la République. À la guillotine !

Vive la Révolution ! Vive la République !
Vive la France !

Download instructions

To download your free resources for 12 Mini French Plays:

Go to: https://www.brilliantpublications.education

You will need to set up a log in with a username, email address and password if you do not already have one for the https://www.brilliantpublications.education website. (Please note: you will need to set up a new account on this website to download your files, even if you already have an account on our main website.)

Your username may contain: **letters**, **numbers** and the special characters *** - _ . @**

You will be asked to confirm your email address by clicking the validation link emailed to you when you register.

Don't forget to check in spam/junk if you do not see an email from us.

We have introduced 2-factor authorisation on this website to make it more secure. This means that whenever you log in, you will be sent a numerical authorisation code by email which you must copy and paste into the welcome page on the website. The authentication code only lasts 1 hour.

Once logged on, choose the French category and click on the cover for 12 Mini French Plays.

Your unique password for the downloads is: **sd2134xc8**

The downloaded filename will be: **12-Mini-French-Plays.zip**

Please note, the password will be changed at regular intervals so make sure you save a copy of the files once you have downloaded them.

If you experience any difficulties with downloading your files, please email info@brilliantpublications.co.uk and we will get back to you as soon as possible.

Depending on the speed of your internet and the size of the download, it may take some time for the download to complete. To avoid problems, please make sure that your computer does not go to sleep during the download.

www.ingramcontent.com/pod-product-compliance
Lightning Source LLC
Chambersburg PA
CBHW080902230426

43663CB00013B/2605